Reflective Teaching

Thomas S. C. Farrell

English Language Teacher Development Series

Thomas S. C. Farrell, Series Editor

Typeset in Janson and Frutiger
by Capitol Communications, LLC, Crofton, Maryland USA
and printed by Gasch Printing, LLC, Odenton, Maryland USA

TESOL International Association
1925 Ballenger Avenue
Alexandria, Virginia 22314 USA
Tel 703-836-0774 • Fax 703-836-7864

Publishing Manager: Carol Edwards
Cover Design: Tomiko Breland
Copyeditor: Jean House

TESOL Book Publications Committee
John I. Liontas, Chair

Maureen S. Andrade	Joe McVeigh
Jennifer Lebedev	Gail Schafers
Robyn L. Brinks Lockwood	Lynn Zimmerman

Project overview: John I. Liontas and Robyn L. Brinks Lockwood
Reviewer: Soonyoung Hwang An

Copyright © 2013 by TESOL International Association

All rights reserved. Copying or further publication of the contents of this work are not permitted without permission of TESOL International Association, except for limited "fair use" for educational, scholarly, and similar purposes as authorized by U.S. Copyright Law, in which case appropriate notice of the source of the work should be given.

Every effort has been made to contact the copyright holders for permission to reprint borrowed material. We regret any oversights that may have occurred and will rectify them in future printings of this work.

ISBN 9781931185776

Contents

Preface

1 Introduction 1

2 Reflective Practice 3

3 Principle 1: Reflective Practice Is Evidence Based 7

4 Principle 2: Reflective Practice Involves Dialogue 21

5 Principle 3: Reflective Practice Links Beliefs and Practices 25

6 Principle 4: Reflective Practice Is a Way of Life 31

7 Conclusion 35

   References 37

About the Author

Thomas S. C. Farrell is Professor of Applied Linguistics at Brock University in Canada. His professional interests include reflective practice and language teacher education and development. His recent books include *Reflecting on Teaching the Four Skills* (2012, Ann Arbor, MI: University of Michigan Press) and *Reflective Writing for Language Teachers* (2013, Sheffield, England: Equinox).

Series Editor's Preface

The English Language Teacher Development (ELTD) Series is a set of short resource books for ESL/EFL teachers that are written in a jargon-free and accessible manner for all types of English language teachers (native and nonnative speakers of English, experienced and novice teachers). The ELTD series is designed to offer teachers a theory-to-practice approach to English language teaching, and each book offers a wide variety of practical teaching approaches and methods for the topic at hand. Each book also offers time for reflections that allow teachers to interact with the materials presented. The books can be used in preservice settings or in-service courses and by individuals who are looking for ways to refresh their practice.

Thomas Farrell's book *Reflective Teaching* outlines four principles of reflective practice that take teachers from just doing reflection to making it a way of being. These principles of reflective practice are *Reflective Practice Is Evidence Based*, *Reflective Practice Involves Dialogue*, *Reflective Practice Links Beliefs and Practices*, and *Reflective Practice Is a Way of Life*. Farrell provides a comprehensive overview of the concept of reflective practice and why it is important for language teachers. *Reflective Teaching* is a valuable addition to the literature in the English language teaching profession.

I am very grateful to the authors who contributed to the ELTD Series for sharing their knowledge and expertise with other TESOL professionals because they have done so willingly and without any compensation to make these short books affordable to language teachers throughout the world. It was truly an honor for me to work with each of these authors as they selflessly gave up their valuable time for the advancement of TESOL.

Thomas S. C. Farrell

1

Introduction

Reflective practice generally means that language teachers systematically examine their beliefs and practices about teaching and learning throughout their careers. In Chapter 1, I outline what reflective practice is and why it is important to do. Then, in the following chapters, I outline four principles of reflective practice. These four principles show teachers how to move from doing reflection to making it a way of being. Chapter 2 outlines Principle 1, *Reflective Practice Is Evidence Based*. Chapter 3 outlines Principle 2, *Reflective Practice Involves Dialogue*. Chapter 4 outlines Principle 3, *Reflective Practice Links Beliefs and Practices*. Chapter 5 outlines Principle 4, *Reflective Practice Is a Way of Life*. Finally, there is a short conclusion to the book.

These principles combined suggest that reflective practice is not a solitary meditative process in which teachers go off alone to ponder what they are doing. Rather, reflective practice as it is presented in this book is a challenging and often demanding process in which teachers are asked to provide evidence about what they are doing. They then use this evidence (often called *data*) to make informed decisions about their work. The process as it is presented in this book also suggests that reflection can be deeper and more rewarding when it is collaborative.

Each chapter has Reflective Breaks, which teachers can use to interact with the contents and draw their own conclusions about reflective practice. These breaks are designed to encourage you, the reader, to interact with the contents of the book and help you begin your own reflections. Because teachers are very busy, it is not necessary to engage with each Reflective Break; rather, you can use them as you see fit, depending on your level of interest and time available to read them. When engaging with the Reflective Breaks, you can use a journal to write down your thoughts, have an internal dialogue with yourself, or talk to another teacher or group of teachers. You can also read the contents of the book and then go back over the breaks alone or with a group of peers to discuss them in order, or choose particular questions to focus on as you review the book. Regardless, this short book is a brief introduction to reflective practice, so it is not all-encompassing. I hope, however, that the contents will encourage English language teachers to read more about the topic.

2

Reflective Practice

I began working in the area of reflective practice, at first informally in the late 1970s and then more formally in the mid-1980s. Since I began, I have always looked at reflective practice as a compass to guide me as I seek direction in my classroom practices. The metaphor of reflection as a compass enables teachers to stop, look, and discover where they are at that moment and then decide where they want to go in the future professionally.

That said, over the years it has seemed that the terms *reflection* and *reflective practice* have become so popular in the field of English language education that using them in such programs is nearly mandatory. Yes, many language educators still agree that some form of reflection is a desirable practice among teachers; however, there is still almost no consensus as to what reflective practice is and which reflective practices actually promote teacher development (Farrell, 2007). Therefore, I will begin by defining reflective practice and then considering why it is important to do before I introduce various principles connected to the concept.

REFLECTIVE BREAK

- What does reflection mean to you?
- What is your metaphor for reflection?
- What is your definition of reflective practice?

What Is Reflective Practice?

Most teachers think about their work either before they teach, while they are teaching, or after they have finished teaching a class. While many think this is reflective practice, it really only consists of fleeting thoughts that are based on hunches, intuition, or even some actions that happened in the class. So much is happening in the classroom during a lesson, though, that teachers cannot really know or see all that transpires. Reflective practice means more than fleeting thoughts before, during, or after a lesson; it means examining what you do in the classroom and why you do it. Reflective practice also means thinking about the beliefs and values related to English language teaching, and seeing if classroom practices are consistent with these beliefs and values. In order to engage in reflective practice, teachers must systematically collect information about their classroom happenings and then analyze and evaluate this information and compare it to their underlying assumptions and beliefs so they can make changes and improvements in their teaching (Farrell, 2007). Reflective practice can also be conducted outside the classroom by looking at the context of teaching, such as when teachers want to see the impact of their teaching on the community or society, or how the community or society impacts their teaching. Questions to consider may include *Who makes the curriculum?* and *What and whose values does the curriculum embody?*

> ### REFLECTIVE BREAK
>
> - Why is the preceding definition, which suggests that teachers collect data about their work, different from the usual way reflective practice is seen?
> - How can collecting data help teachers make informed decisions about their practice?
> - How can teachers collect data about their practice?
> - Why is reflecting on practice important for a teacher?

Why Is Reflective Practice Important?

Teachers may ask why they should reflect on their practice beyond the quick after-class muse, which may lead to perceptions such as "That was a good class!" or "That was a bad class!" or "The students were not very responsive today!" Although these musings may act as a necessary starting point for most teachers, they do not produce any real evidence whether the perceptions they lead to are correct or not. For example, some teachers end class happy because they think it went well. Conversely, they may feel unhappy at the end of a class because they have perceived it to have gone badly and, worse, they spent a good deal of time preparing for that particular class. Some teachers base their initial perceptions of their teaching on the way students respond (e.g., yawning) or do not respond during class. This kind of evidence may not lead to correct interpretations of the teachers' perceptions because yawning may have nothing to do with the class and the teaching and everything to do with a student's tiredness. Likewise, if students do not respond to teaching and lessons, teachers should investigate why they were not responsive without becoming too defensive. Teachers need to know why some classes seem to go well and others not so well, and how they define what *well* means. This investigation is called *evidence-based* reflective practice. As such, teachers need to compile solid data about what is really happening in their classrooms rather than what they think is happening. Reflective practice is important because it helps teachers make more informed decisions about their teaching—decisions that are based on concrete evidence systematically collected over a period of time.

Reflective Break

- When teachers think about their teaching, they usually come up with statements such as "My lesson went well" or "My students seemed not to be interested today" or "I did not like that lesson," and then they make decisions about how they will conduct future classes. Would this be considered reflective practice? If yes, why? If not, why not?

Principles of Reflective Practice

In the remainder of this short book, I outline four principles of reflective practice:

Principle 1: Reflective Practice Is Evidence Based

Principle 2: Reflective Practice Involves Dialogue

Principle 3: Reflective Practice Explores Beliefs and Practices

Principle 4: Reflective Practice Is a Way of Life

> **REFLECTIVE BREAK**
>
> - What is your understanding of each of these four principles?

3

Principle 1: Reflective Practice Is Evidence Based

My early work (in the late 1970s) in reflective practice was very tentative, but I realized that I was always interested in—and even worried about—the impact my classes were having (or not having) on students' learning. For example, I remember wondering in the middle of one particular class if the group work I had assigned was actually useful for them or just easy for me to monitor and easier than teaching particular grammar items. Yes, I had read all the latest theories at that time, especially those suggesting that it is better not to teach grammar overtly but instead to provide opportunities for students to use the language in class. I followed this method even though I often wondered if the students in my classes were at times just practicing their mistakes. Also at that time, I had read that it is best not to correct each mistake because it threatens students' motivation to speak, so I let them practice speaking and went over common errors only at the end of each lesson. I remember thinking at the time that it was fine for me as a teacher because it was easier to set up the groups and let them speak—my interpretation of the so-called communicative language teaching approach. As time went by, though, at the end of the 1970s and into the early 1980s, I decided to try to figure it out myself by thinking about what I was doing in a more systematic manner. I began by reading some of John Dewey's work on *reflective inquiry*, which seemed to be the most suitable method for the systematic reflective practice I was interested in.

Reflective Break

- Have you ever stopped for a moment during a class and wondered what was happening?

Reflective Inquiry

Early in the 20th century, the respected U.S. educator John Dewey suggested that one main aim of education is to help people acquire habits of reflection so they can engage in intelligent thought and action rather than routine thought and action (I take most of the following ideas from Dewey's important book *How We Think*, published in 1933). Dewey's work was situated in the post–Great Depression U.S. society, and he felt the need for a thinking citizenry in a democratic society. For him, this ideal was the larger purpose of reflective inquiry. Dewey (1933) first outlined what reflective inquiry was not, which is useful given the current lack of clarity and definitional problems associated with the concept of reflective practice. He said that it is not just mulling over interesting things, which seems to be a common misperception of reflective thinking today, and he was concerned about routine thinking whereby actions are guided by impulse, tradition, or authority. Dewey (1933) observed that teachers who do not bother to think intelligently about their work become slaves to routine, and he noted that one of the main challenges of learning was learning how to think intelligently: "While we cannot learn or be taught to think, we do have to learn how to think well, especially how to acquire the general habits of reflecting" (p. 35).

Reflective Break

- How do you start your classes each day?
- How do you end your classes each day?
- How do you go through the textbook?
- Do you think that teachers should follow a routine?

In answer to the Reflective Break questions above, some teachers may say that routine is necessary. This belief came up recently for me, when I was asked how I teach the same classes each year. I answered without hesitation that I do not teach classes, I teach students, so there is no routine for me; my practice depends on how each student reacts or does not react or how I react or do not react as each class progresses. So Dewey may have been correct to suggest that teachers should be on guard against blindly following routine, because if teachers follow routine then they will certainly be teaching classes rather than students. Dewey (1933) noted

> *Reflection emancipates us from merely impulsive and merely routine activity, it enables us to direct our activities with foresight and to plan according to ends-in-view or purposes of which we are aware, to act in deliberate and intentional fashion, to know what we are about when we act. (p. 17)*

Thus, Dewey (1933) considered reflective practice to be intentional, systematic inquiry that is disciplined and will ultimately lead to change and professional growth for teachers.

Dewey's legacy is important because it moved the concept of reflection far beyond everyday simple wonderings about a situation (or mulling over something without taking action) to a more rigorous form of thinking, whereby a teacher systematically investigates a perceived problem in order to discover a solution. That said, Dewey (1933) did not consider a problem to be an error or a mistake but rather a puzzling, curious, inviting, and engaging issue for a teacher to investigate. Many years later, Zeichner and Liston (1996) returned to Dewey's original ideas when they distinguished between routine action and reflective action and suggested that, for teachers, "routine action is guided primarily by tradition, external authority and circumstance" whereas reflective action "entails the active, persistent and careful consideration of any belief or supposed form of knowledge" (p. 24).

Dewey (1933) encouraged teachers to make informed decisions based on systematic and conscious reflections rather than fleeting thoughts about teaching, and he maintained that when teachers combine these systematic reflections with their actual teaching experiences, then they can become more aware, which can lead to professional development. Thus, Dewey was advocating early for a form of evidence-based teaching.

> ### REFLECTIVE BREAK
>
> - What is the difference between a teacher thinking about how a class went and collecting evidence about how a class went?
> - How can a teacher collect evidence about his or her teaching?

Evidence-Based Reflective Practice

For me, the implication of Dewey's work is that reflective practice is evidence based: Teachers collect data or evidence about their work and then reflect on this evidence to make informed decisions about their practice. For example, if a teacher says a class has been a bad class or a good class, my questions are *How do you know?* and *Where is the evidence?* If the teacher replies that she noticed that students looked bored or were yawning, I ask *How can we be sure that this look or yawn has anything to do with your teaching?* Students may have been tired or have had a difficult class prior to this particular one. It is important to collect evidence from sources other than fleeting perceptions based on brief musings.

Engaging in evidence-based reflective practice enables teachers to articulate to themselves and others what they do, how they do it, why they do it, and what the impact of their teaching is on student learning. Engaging in such reflective practice may result in either affirming current practices or making changes, but these changes will not be based on impulse, tradition, or the like; rather, they will emerge from analysis of concrete evidence. Evidence-based reflective practice is centered on five important questions teachers ask themselves about their practice:

1. What do I do?
2. How do I do it?
3. Why do I do it?

4. What is the result?
5. Will I change anything based on the answers to the above questions?

By systematically collecting data to answer these questions, teachers can engage in evidence-based reflective practice.

What Do I Do?

One way for teachers to begin is to reflect on recent teaching practices or experiences that happened in their classrooms and caused them to stop and think about their teaching. For example, teachers may have both positive and negative experiences that they do not plan or even anticipate but that they clearly remember after class and even weeks later. For example, a teacher may make a sudden change in a lesson plan during class: Because the teacher perceives that the lesson may be going better than anticipated, rather than move on to originally scheduled activities the teacher may decide to extend a successful activity until the end of the lesson because of the overall positive student response to it. Conversely, something may happen in a lesson that can be problematic or persuades the teacher into doing something he or she would not normally do, such as abandoning a particular activity or disciplining a student. The point is to recall incidents that the teacher thinks were significant events. By recalling, describing, and analyzing such incidents, teachers can begin to explore their deeper held assumptions about effective teaching practices.

Alternatively, teachers can construct a case study related to their teaching. Case studies usually describe and outline the kind of dilemmas that some teachers may encounter while teaching, and they allow for bridging the gap between theory and practice, which is the core of reflective practice. When a teacher discusses a case, he defines the problems that the case presents, clarifies particular issues, looks at alternatives, and chooses a particular course of action to follow. The following examples of case studies could be used as part of a reflection activity (from Richards & Farrell, 2005):

- an account of the problems or joys a novice teacher experienced during his or her first few months of teaching

- an account of observation of one high-achieving student and one low-achieving student over the course of a semester in order to compare their patterns of classroom participation
- an account based on a teacher's journal of all of the student grouping problems she had to deal with in a conversation class
- an account of how a teacher made use of lesson plans for a fixed number of classes

> ### REFLECTIVE BREAK
>
> - Describe any one issue that you would be interested in exploring related to your teaching. This may be something that goes well or not so well.
> - Why did you choose to focus on this issue?
> - Now describe the issue in as much detail as you can.
> - Describe how the issue relates to your own teaching beliefs and values.
> - Explore one or more of the cases outlined above.

How Do I Do It?

To determine how they do what they do, teachers must collect evidence about teaching rather than just thinking about what they do. Teachers can gather evidence from many sources: self-reflection, their students' views, and their colleagues' reflections. The point is that teachers cast a wide net when compiling this evidence to avoid being too biased in their explorations.

Self-Reflection

Teachers can self-reflect, of course, and this should be the starting point of reflective practice. Tools that can help teachers in self-reflection include keeping teaching journals and recording lessons. Teaching journals are a good way to begin self-reflection because they provide teachers with a written record of various aspects of their practice. The very act of writing means that teachers must slow their thoughts momentarily to think about their practices. When teachers write regularly in teaching journals, they can accumulate information that, on later review, interpretation, and reflection can assist them in gaining a deeper understanding of their work (Farrell, 2007, 2013). Teachers who are beginning to reflect on their work without any particular focus can write regularly for a period of time in response to such prompts as *What did you notice in your classes today or this week?* and *What professional issues are of interest to you today or this week?* They can look for patterns, and then after a month or so decide on a further focus for their reflections. Or they may have already decided on a focus sooner, during their month of journaling, and write only about this topic. Either way, it is important for teachers to write regularly (possibly after each lesson, initially) to describe their reactions (and those of their students), feelings, and thoughts because teachers may become too selective later in what they want to remember (see Farrell, 2013, for more details on writing as reflective practice). In addition, the Internet offers opportunities for teachers to share their teaching journals on a wider scale by keeping online teaching journals and web logs.

Reflective Break

- Focus on a recent issue you found important in your teaching. This can be something that worked well for you or did not work at all.

- Write about this issue for a few weeks as you observe how it works (or does not work) in classes. Did you find any patterns emerging from your writing?

- What interpretations do you make from these patterns, and what do these interpretations mean to you as a teacher?

Teachers can also record their lessons on audio or video to aid self-reflection. It is nearly impossible for teachers to be aware of everything that occurs while they are teaching a class, but recording classes provides an accurate picture of what actually happened during the lesson. When teachers are in the middle of teaching classes, they are monitoring their students, making decisions about what they will say, and thinking ahead about where they want the lesson to go. In fact, many teachers report that they are on autopilot while teaching and find it difficult to remember exactly what happened even minutes after the lesson. When teachers record their lessons, however, they can play them back to hear or see, for example, how much teacher talk they engage in and compare this to their lesson objectives. If they notice that they talk more than their students, but the lesson objective was to get the students talking, then they have evidence to make a change for the next lesson. In addition, teachers can use recordings to explore how many questions they ask and what types of questions they favor; what instructions they give, how they give them, and their students' reactions to these instructions; and how they give feedback to their students as well as their students' reactions to such feedback. Video can show a teacher's *action zone*, that is, who the teacher interacts with most and where the teacher usually stands or sits in class, as well as what the students are doing in the class. In fact, the list of what teachers can review from an audio or video recording is endless. All of these elements are difficult to monitor while a teacher is teaching a class but can be reviewed later for reflection.

> ### REFLECTIVE BREAK
>
> - Record one of your classes and play it back. What do you notice first?
>
> - What issues did you see or hear that you would like to reflect on further?
>
> - Review the recording with a colleague and discuss what you see or hear.
>
> - What are the main differences between what you observe and what your colleague observes?

Student Reflections

Teachers can also obtain data about their teaching from their students. They can use the more traditional end-of-term student evaluations, or they can use concept maps. In many schools, administrators have built-in end-of-semester student evaluations in which students are asked to respond to a teacher's teaching and the lessons over the course of a semester or year. Students are usually given a checklist developed by the school, on which they answer standardized multiple-choice questions about the teacher, his or her teaching, and the lessons. Some forms also allow for open-ended responses from the students. Teachers can also ask their students for feedback during the semester regarding particular lessons. For example, at the end of each class teachers can ask their students what they thought the lesson was about, what was difficult for them, and what was easy for them, or they can ask their students to keep learning journals in which they regularly reflect on their lessons.

Concept maps show relationships between concepts in a type of network where any concept or idea can be connected to any other. Because concept maps are a useful indication of what people know about a topic, they can be a helpful reflection device for both teachers and students when gathering information about teaching and learning. For English language teachers, concept maps can be used to measure cognitive change in their students as a result of taking their course or as a result of one particular lesson. For students, concept maps can be used to reflect on their learning because they demonstrate how students relate (or do not relate) new concepts to their current knowledge. Teachers can use concept mapping as a diagnostic pre-activity or a way to prepare students for a particular topic. They can also be used during lessons as a record of what students are learning or at the end of a lesson to see what concepts students have understood in that particular lesson. Farrell (2007) has suggested that in order to use concept mapping effectively, teachers should first provide a *sample concept map* on the board because this technique may not be familiar to all students; also, teachers should model their reflective thinking by *thinking aloud* about the construction of the map as they draw their concepts of a particular topic.

> **REFLECTIVE BREAK**
>
> - Construct a concept map about how to teach a particular language skill.
>
> - Now get your students to construct their own concept maps of the same language skill you are teaching and compare it to what you constructed.
>
> - Have your students construct a concept map at the beginning of each lesson and the end of each lesson, and compare both. This way, students will be asked to reflect before and after each lesson.

The following is a narrative account from an English language teacher who decided to engage in reflective practice after attending a workshop I gave on the topic. I use the teacher's own words to illustrate how powerful reflective practice can be and what can happen when teachers take a short amount of time to ask students what they think about a lesson. This narrative also demonstrates how asking students reflective questions makes them reflective learners, so reflection takes place for both teachers and students. The teacher starts by stating that after attending the workshop on reflective practice she realized that she did not always ask her students about their learning in her lessons; what follows demonstrates what the teacher did to incorporate reflective practice into her lessons.

> *I realized [after the workshop] I have never given my students the opportunity to consciously reflect on what they learned in class. So I made a decision to start class reflections with one of my beginner classes. I chose them because the students are always thanking me for my teaching, which made me assume that they were happy and were learning. So at the end of our class I gave them a survey to complete. The survey was brief and based on what I heard at the workshop where teachers can ask students to reflect at the end of each lesson by asking them three simple questions: what was the class about? What did you learn? What was difficult? The most interesting observation was*

that for the question, "What was class about?" Almost every student answered that the class was "interesting." And for the question, "What did you learn?" they'd answer: "Thank you for your teaching," or "You are a good teacher." The next class I did the same survey with them again and as I walked about looking over shoulders I noticed they were repeating the same answers. So I explained to them that the questions were not about how the class was or about my teaching, but about their experience as learners. I continued to do the same survey after each class and slowly their reflections became clearer and more critical. Finally after about four more lessons they mentioned that they had some difficulty understanding my pronunciation. It was actually comforting for me to read that because they brought something to my attention that I had not realized and I decided to speak more slowly and enunciate more clearly. In the follow-up surveys the students mentioned that my pronunciation was easier to understand. Reflective practice really works and is simple to use.

REFLECTIVE BREAK

- Do you ask your students what they think about a lesson or lessons you delivered?

- At the end of each class for a month, follow the procedures this teacher used and ask your students to answer the following questions:
  — What was the class about?
  — What did you learn?
  — What was easy for you?
  — What was difficult for you?
  — What other comments would you like to make about today's lesson?

Colleagues' Reflections

Teachers can engage in classroom observation to develop more awareness of the principles and decision making that inspire their teaching. They can do this alone, either in self-reflection (explained earlier) where they write about the lesson afterward or by recording the lesson (also explained earlier) and then reviewing the recording afterward so that they better understand their own instructional practices and make decisions about practices they wish to change. Teachers can also obtain their colleagues' feedback by having a peer observe their teaching. Peers may decide to observe each other teach and then share feedback. Before each observation, they should understand exactly what they want observed, so they should meet beforehand to discuss the goal of the observation and possibly a task for the observer to accomplish. The peers also should agree on observation procedures and types of instruments (quantitative, qualitative, or both) to be used during the sessions and arrange a schedule for the observations. When classroom observations are carried out with peers, teachers may be able to gain more self-knowledge about the strategies other teachers use.

> ### REFLECTIVE BREAK
>
> - Arrange to have a peer observe your class, and ask him or her to look at some of the following issues in your teaching (from Richards & Farrell, 2005):
>   — *teacher's time management*, the allotment of time to different activities during the lesson
>   — *students' performance on tasks*, their strategies, procedures, and interaction patterns
>   — *teacher's action zone*, the extent to which the teacher interacted with some students more frequently than others during a lesson
>   — *use of the textbook*, the extent to which a teacher used the textbook during a lesson and the types of departures made from it

— *pair work*, the way students completed a pair-work task, the responses they made during the task, and the type of language they used

— *group work*, students' use of their first language (L1) versus the second language (L2) during group work, students' time-on-task during group work, and the dynamics of group activities

— *classroom interaction*, the different types of seating arrangements that provide or block opportunities for more student participation and language development

— *lesson structure*, the nature and impact of the learning activities

— *classroom communication*, the communication patterns evident, including the teacher's use of questioning, that either promote or block opportunities for learning

Why Do I Do It?

The answer to this particular question will depend on teachers' beliefs regarding teaching and learning English. Once teachers have articulated their beliefs, they then look at their classroom practices to see if these beliefs remain valid or if they want to change their practices in light of their articulated beliefs (see Chapter 5 on Principle 3 for more details on teacher beliefs). Teachers can also consider how others address similar issues and if this has an impact on what they will implement in their classrooms in the future.

What Is the Result?

Teachers teach with the hope that students will learn something from them. After examining specific issues related to their practices, teachers can ask questions such as

- What happened that was expected or surprising?
- What theories about teaching or personal experiences with learning are revealed in the data I have collected?

- How do these theories relate to my stated beliefs and attitudes?
- What are the consequences of my actions?
- What exactly are my students learning?

Will I Change Anything?

The final question a teacher can ask within evidence-based reflective practice concerns action: Will I change anything based on the answers to these questions? The answer to this question will, of course, depend on what answers the teacher has discovered to the preceding questions (*What Do I Do? How Do I Do It? Why Do I Do It?* and *What Is the Result?*). The point is for the teacher to link the information gathered—whatever insights he or she has gained from the reflective process as a whole—to whatever changes (if any) he or she wants to make in his or her teaching.

4

Principle 2: Reflective Practice Involves Dialogue

Teachers can engage in evidence-based reflective practice by themselves, and this is a good starting point for all teachers. While teachers are self-reflecting, however, they may encounter issues or situations that may be unpleasant and so avoid these and become biased in their reflections, choosing to explore only topics that do not upset them. In other words, teachers can become biased in what they self-reflect on, so they may need to be challenged if they become too comfortable with their teaching or if they have not asked themselves difficult questions about what they do. As such, Principle 2 suggests that reflective practice is informed by some kind of dialogue with the self but mostly with others so that teachers can have a deeper understanding of themselves as teachers. As Kumaravadivelu (2012) has noted, "Teaching is a reflective activity which at once shapes and is shaped by the doing of theorizing which in turn is bolstered by the collaborative process of dialogic inquiry" (p. 95).

> ### REFLECTIVE BREAK
> - How can dialogue with others help teachers critically reflect on practice?

Reflection as Dialogue

Reflective practice through dialogue begins with the self, when a teacher engages in internal dialogue about his or her own practice. A teacher can begin this internal dialogue by telling his or her own teaching story, such as in an autobiography, which can be analyzed later for that teacher's stated or implied beliefs, assumptions, and values about teaching and learning English. By telling their stories, teachers can make better sense of seemingly random experiences because they hold insider knowledge, especially personal intuitive knowledge, expertise, and experience that is based on their accumulated years as language educators teaching in schools and classrooms. These self-reflection stories can provide a rich source of teacher-generated information that allows teachers to reflect on how they arrived where they are today; how they conduct practice; and the underlying assumptions, values, and beliefs that have ruled their past and current practices (see also Chapter 6 on Principle 4, Reflective Practice Is a Way of Life).

> ### REFLECTIVE BREAK
>
> - Tell your teaching story so far.
> - What insight can you get from your story, and where you are today as a teacher?

Expanding the Dialogue

The dialogue with self can be expanded to include others, such as through a critical friendship or a teacher reflection group. For example, if a teacher wants to dialogue with another peer, he or she can choose to enter a critical friendship, team-teaching, or peer-coaching relationship whereby both teachers collaborate to encourage dialogue and reflection in order to improve the quality of language teaching and learning in some way. In a teacher reflection group, members discuss and reflect on practice. Following is an explanation of each of these types of relationships.

In a *critical friendship*, a trusted colleague gives advice to a teacher as a friend rather than as a consultant in order to develop the reflective abilities of the teacher who is conducting her own reflections. In this collaborative relationship, dialogue between the teacher and the friend includes questioning and even confronting the trusted other in order to explore teaching and also being heard in a sympathetic but constructively critical way. In this way, dialogues within the critical friendship stimulate reflection and also clarify and extend reflection beyond descriptive levels to more conceptual and critical levels. When teachers reflect on the conceptual level of reflection, they focus their reflections on the theory behind their classroom practices. At this level of reflection, teachers can also look into alternative practices (depending on their students' needs) they might use based on their descriptions and analysis of their reasons for doing what they are doing. Critical reflection, which is an even deeper level of reflection, encourages teachers to justify the work they do and reflect within the broader context of society, focusing on the moral, ethical, and sociopolitical issues associated with their practices.

Team teaching is another type of arrangement, whereby two or more teachers cooperate as equals as they take responsibility for planning, teaching, and evaluating a class, a series of classes, or a whole course. Of course, teams should realize that team teaching is just that: a team—not two individuals—planning the lessons, deciding and preparing the activities, delivering the lessons, and evaluating the effectiveness of the lessons. *Peer coaching*, on the other hand, focuses specifically on the process of teaching and on how two teachers can collaborate to help one or both improve some aspect of their teaching through dialogue. A peer-coaching arrangement usually takes place so that the observed teacher can develop new knowledge and skills and a deeper awareness of his own teaching. For peer coaching to be successful, each participant must recognize that he or she has a specific role to play in the relationship.

Teachers can also join a *teacher reflection group*, either within their own institution or with teachers from other institutions. The teacher reflection group meets regularly to discuss and reflect on practice. These group discussions can act to break the sense of isolation many teachers say they feel when they talk about their teaching, and the group can also complement individual members' strengths and compensate for each member's limitations. When teachers gather in such groups, it is important to allot roles to each member, focus on particular discussion topics for each meeting, and develop a nonthreatening environment in which all the members gain supportive feedback from their peers. Thus, when language teachers come together in such a group, they can help each other to articulate their thoughts about their work so that they can all grow professionally together. Because teachers are very busy, one factor that should be addressed with these groups is time. I have worked with several groups whose members were initially worried about the time that meeting would take from their professional and personal lives, but as they began dialoging, they realized the value of meeting. As one group member recently noted, "I admit that when we first talked about giving up my Saturday morning I felt a bit concerned about whether I had made the right choice but in the end felt it was time well spent."

Reflective Break

- Look at the collaborative arrangements mentioned (critical friendships, team teaching, peer coaching, and teacher reflection groups). Which of these would work best for you and why?

5

Principle 3: Reflective Practice Links Beliefs and Practices

Principle 3 argues that reflective practice can be used as a tool to explore teacher beliefs and compare them to classroom practices so that theory is directly linked to practice. This principle is influenced by Dewey's (1933) work, which suggests that teachers should examine what is actual and occurring (*theories-in-use*) in their practice and compare this to their beliefs (*espoused theories*) about learning and teaching. This productive tension between espoused theories and theories-in-use provides teachers with the opportunity to systematically look at their practices so that they can deepen their understanding of what they do and thus come to new insights about their students, their teaching, and themselves (Freeman, personal communication). As Dewey (1933) noted, growth comes from a "reconstruction of experience" (p. 87). By reflecting on these experiences, teachers can reconstruct their own approaches to teaching.

Teacher Beliefs

Reflective practice recognizes the power of a teacher's assumptions, values, and beliefs because these espoused theories of teaching influence the instructional judgments and decisions made in classrooms. As Borg (2003) points out, "teachers are active, thinking decision-makers who make instructional choices by drawing on complex practically-oriented, personalized, and context-sensitive networks of knowledge, thoughts, and beliefs" (p. 81). Not many language teachers are aware of their espoused theories (beliefs), however, and to what extent their beliefs are reflected or not in their classroom practices (Farrell, 2007).

Thus, when teachers engage in systematic reflective practice, they can begin to uncover their beliefs. As Knezedivc (2001) has suggested, awareness of beliefs and practices is a necessary starting point in reflections because teachers cannot develop "unless we are aware of who we are and what we do" and "developing awareness is a process of reducing the discrepancy between what we do and what we think we do" (p. 10). When attempting to articulate their espoused theories about teaching and learning, teachers can also examine the sources of such beliefs to explore what and who has influenced the development of such beliefs and if they remain valid after such reflections. As Woods (1996) maintains, language teachers must be on guard so as not to "claim allegiance to beliefs consistent with what they perceive as the current teaching paradigm rather than consistent with their unmonitored beliefs and their behaviour in class" (p. 71). Once teachers have reflected on their belief systems, they can then examine how these beliefs are translated (or not) into actual classroom practice.

Zahorik (1986) came up with the following three conceptions of teaching, which can help teachers identify their own approach to language teaching.

> Science/Research, *which is derived from research and supported by experimentation. Here teaching is informed by a tested model of learning, and if teachers learn specific acts of teaching (such as effective questioning, and effective wait-time), then they will be successful teachers. Also, effective teachers are observed and their actions documented. Effective teachers are chosen as a result of their students' high scores on tests.*
>
> Theory/Values, *in which teaching is based on what ought to work or what is morally right to do. Reflective teaching is an example of a values approach to teaching, as is a learner-centered approach to teaching because teachers value these approaches. There is no empirical research information to back up any of the conceptions in the theory/values approach.*
>
> Art/Craft, *in which each teaching situation is distinct and each teacher decides what to do based on his or her teaching skills and personality. The teacher does not follow any one method and chooses from a range of options to teach.*

Reflective Break

- What are your beliefs about how a language is learned (e.g., memorization, practice speaking, grammar drills)?
- What are your beliefs about how teachers should teach language?
- Where do your beliefs come from?
- What is your role as a language teacher?
- What are the roles of your students?
- If you had the power, how would you design your ideal English language classroom?
- Look at the three conceptions of teaching from Zahorik (1986) above and decide which classification best fits your approach to language teaching.

Beliefs and Practices

After teachers articulate their espoused theories (what teachers *say* they do in class), they then compare these with their theories-in-use (what they actually *do* in class) to see if there is convergence or divergence between both. By systematically reflecting on the comparison of what teachers say they do (stated beliefs) and what they actually do (classroom practices), they can develop understanding of what they want to do and accomplish in terms of students' learning by constructing *theories-of-action, theories-in-action,* and *theories-for-action*. In other words, it is a helpful reflective exercise for teachers to state (or write in a journal) what they think they do in class, then they may record or ask a colleague to observe them teach, and compare the two. For example, a teacher might state how he or she gives instructions in class and then record the class or ask a colleague to observe. The colleague would note the places the teacher gives instructions, or the teacher would transcribe these from the recording, to discover whether there is convergence or divergence between what the teacher says he does and what he actually does.

Some teachers may say the core of reflective practice involves teachers continually seeking to compare their espoused theories, or stated beliefs, with their theories-in-use, or practices, so that they can ultimately construct their own theories-of-action and theories-for-action. What teachers say they do (their espoused theories) and what they actually do in the classroom (their theories-in-action) are not always the same, though. Indeed, a recent review of research on beliefs demonstrated that language teachers' belief systems do not always correspond with their classroom practices (Basturkmen, 2012). By systematically reflecting on the comparison of what teachers say they do and what they actually do, or if there is an alignment between beliefs and practices, teachers can develop a better understanding of what they want to do in their classrooms. The point of reflecting on the alignment between beliefs and practices is not to suggest that one method of teaching is better than any other; rather, exploring beliefs and corresponding classroom practices can help clarify how teachers can implement changes to their approaches to teaching and learning over time. In this way, teachers ultimately seek to construct their own theories-of, -in, and -for-action.

To construct theories-of, -in, and -for-action, teachers should be aware of the differences between reflecting-on, -in, and -for-action. Teachers can reflect after, before, and during class, and ideally, all these moments of reflection are linked to each other as teachers reflect on, in, and for action. When teachers reflect after class, this is called *reflection-on-action*. In order to reflect on action, teachers can record their classes and review these later as well as have someone observe them as they teach and then discuss these observations later (this will be discussed in more detail below). For example, if a lesson does not go so well, the teacher will want to find out the reasons why; with equal interest, if the lesson goes well, the teacher will want to know why it went well. Many of the activities in this book help teachers reflect after their classes, and the framework that follows offers specific tools for teachers to consider when reflecting-on-action.

When teachers reflect before class, this is called *reflection-for-action*. Reflection-for-action is a process by which teachers prepare a detailed lesson plan that is based on the needs of the students and the knowledge the teacher has gained from reflecting on what happened in previous classes (Farrell, 2007). This type of reflection-for-action is proactive so that teachers are able to prepare for future action.

Reflection-in-action is more difficult to capture because it happens when teachers reflect during class. Reflection-in-action (Schön, 1983, 1987) happens when teachers are teaching and something occurs that upsets their routine. Thus, there is a sequence of moments in a process of reflection-in-action in which the practitioner attempts to solve a problem as follows:

- A situation develops that triggers spontaneous, routine responses (such as in knowing-in-action): For example, a student cannot answer an easy grammar question, such as identifying a grammar structure, that she was able to answer during the previous class.

- Routine responses by the teacher (i.e., what the teacher has always done) do not produce a routine response and instead produce a surprise for the teacher: The teacher starts to explain how the student had already explained this grammar structure in the previous class, so the teacher wonders why the current inability is the case. The teacher asks the student if anything is the matter, and the student says that she forgets the answer.

- This surprise response gets the teacher's attention and leads to reflection within an action: The teacher reacts quickly to try to find out why the student suddenly forgets a grammar structure the teacher knows the student has no trouble understanding. The teacher can ask the student directly to explain what is happening.

- Reflection now gives rise to on-the-spot experimentation by the teacher: The student may or may not explain. The teacher will take some measures (depending on reaction or no reaction) to help solve the problem. He may ignore the situation, empathize with the student, help the student answer the question by modeling answers, and so forth.

Many experienced teachers, for example, will notice when a class, although it may have been carefully planned, falls flat, perhaps because the students are not focused enough to study (e.g., they may be upset over something that happened in a previous class), so the teacher may want to take some action. Because novice teachers may not have built up sufficient knowledge about teaching routines, they may find such action difficult to implement; with time and experience reflecting on their teaching, though, they will be able to notice these classroom routines and changes that may occur while they are teaching, especially if they engage in systematic reflection after class. By reflecting-on, -in, and -for-action; comparing their articulated beliefs about teaching and learning; and then monitoring their teaching by regularly comparing beliefs and practices, teachers can begin to construct theories-of-action and theories-for-action. As Stanley (1998) suggests, these types of activities are what "reflective practitioners do when they look at their work in the moment (reflection-in-action) or in retrospect (reflection-on-action) in order to examine the reasons and beliefs underlying their actions and generate alternative actions for the future" (p. 585). Indeed, throughout their careers, many language teachers are expected to learn about their own profession not by studying their own experiences but by studying the findings of outside experts. By engaging in lifelong reflective practice as outlined in this book (see the following section), language teachers can become producers of their own theories and knowledge that are grounded in real classrooms.

Reflective Break

- What is your understanding of reflection-in-action, reflection-on-action, and reflection-for-action?
- How can reflecting on beliefs and practices help teachers construct their own theories-of-action, theories-in-action, and theories-for-action?
- How can teachers become producers of their own knowledge?

6

Principle 4: Reflective Practice Is a Way of Life

Principle 4 suggests that reflective practice should not be considered just a method to explore teaching. Rather, it is more than a method: It is a *way of life*. Yes, reflective practice suggests that teachers should take a step back every now and then to systematically explore their practice. Teachers also should be aware of what is happening throughout their careers, as well as throughout the teaching day. In fact, engaging in reflective practice as a way of life, as Oberg and Blades (1990) maintained, "lies not in the theory it allows us to develop (about practice or reflection) but the evolution of ourselves as a teacher. Its focus is life; we continually return to our place of origin, but it is not the place we left" (p. 179). Thus, teachers can engage in reflective practice at any stage of their careers and at any time of the teaching day as they continue to construct their own personal theories of teaching and improve their instructional practice.

> ### REFLECTIVE BREAK
> - What is your understanding of the principle Reflective Practice Is a Way of Life?

Reflection as a Way of Life

Surely, newly graduated and novice English language teachers may assume that because they have just been trained and educated in all the up-to-date approaches, methods, and techniques in their particular program, there is no need to reflect on their practice. The call in this section for ongoing reflection, however, does not mean that teachers have been inadequately trained or educated in their initial teacher education programs; rather, it is a response to the facts that not everything a language teacher needs to know can be provided at the preservice level (or even in in-service workshops) and that the knowledge base of teaching is constantly changing, with new theories and approaches that will need to be examined in a professional manner rather than blindly followed. Indeed, Kumaravadivelu (2003) has suggested that English language teachers should enter into "a continual process of self-reflection and self-renewal" so that they can "construct their own personal theory of teaching" (p. 17).

Teachers who engage in lifelong reflective practice can develop a deeper understanding of their teaching, assess their professional growth, develop informed decision-making skills, and become proactive and confident in their teaching and possibly their personal life as well. Reflective practice as a way of life tends to move beyond reflecting on classroom actions to include reflection on identity: who teachers are.

Teacher Identity

Teacher role identity includes beliefs, values, and emotions about many aspects of teaching and being a teacher. Reflecting on teacher role identity allows language educators and teachers a useful lens into the *who* of teaching and how teachers construct and reconstruct their views of their roles as language teachers and themselves in relation to their peers and their context. Burns and Richards (2009) suggested that identity "reflects how individuals see themselves and how they enact their *roles* [emphasis added] within different settings" (p. 5). For teachers, professional self-image is usually seen and balanced with a variety of roles that include all the functional roles a teacher uses while performing his or her duties. For example, recently Farrell (2011) identified 16 main role identities for experienced ESL teachers in Canada, divided into three major role identity clusters: teacher-as-manager (attempts to control everything that happens in classroom), teacher-as-professional (dedicated to the work; continuously upgrading), and teacher-as-acculturator (helps students get accustomed to life outside class), the latter of which may be distinctive to English language teachers. Farrell (2011) suggests that by engaging in reflective practice, teachers may become more aware of their identity roles, as well as how those roles have been shaped over time and by whom, and how they need to be nurtured during the course of a career.

> ### REFLECTIVE BREAK
>
> - Which of the metaphors in the three major role identity clusters (manager, professional, or acculturator) above do you think best represents your role as a language teacher?

Reflection as an everyday way of life is governed by teachers' unwillingness to accept *what is* and to systematically question what they see in their professional practice. Reflective practice as a way of life also means that the teacher will have to possess certain qualities to enable constant questioning of their practice. Dewey (1933) identified three attributes or characteristics of reflective individuals that I think are still important today for teachers: open-mindedness, responsibility, and wholeheartedness. Open-mindedness is a desire to listen to more than one side of an issue and to give attention to alternative views. Responsibility means careful consideration of the consequences to which an action leads. Wholeheartedness implies that teachers can overcome fears and uncertainties to critically evaluate their practice in order to make meaningful change.

> ### REFLECTIVE BREAK
>
> - Look at Dewey's three characteristics above and see what degree of each you possess.
> - What levels of these characteristics do you possess as a teacher now? High? Medium? Low?
> - Which of these characteristics do you need to develop more as you continue as a teacher?
> - Can you think of other desirable characteristics a reflective practitioner should possess?

In addition, Zeichner and Liston (1996, p. 6) have suggested five key features of a reflective teacher. A reflective teacher

- examines, frames, and attempts to solve dilemmas in classroom practice
- is aware of and questions the assumptions and values he or she brings to teaching
- is attentive to the institutional and cultural contexts in which he or she teaches
- takes part in curriculum development and is involved in school change efforts
- takes responsibility for his or her own professional development.

REFLECTIVE BREAK

- Look at Zeichner and Liston's five key features of a reflective teacher, listed above, and assess how closely you follow, or do not follow, each and also comment on each of these features.

- Try to give examples of each of these features from your recent reflections, or outline how you will incorporate each of these features into your future reflections on your practice.

7

Conclusion

Reflective practice as it is outlined in this short book is much more than taking a few minutes to think about teaching, which most teachers do regularly after a class or on the way home from school. Reflective practice as it is outlined here is evidence based because it involves systematically gathering data about teaching and using this information to make informed decisions about practice.

Reflective practice also means teachers enter a dialogue with themselves and other teachers so that they can reach a new level of awareness and understanding of their practice. This dialogue can occur with the self, a critical friend, or a teacher reflection group. The dialogue is supportive and at the same time sympathetically challenging so that individual teachers can reach a level of awareness of what they do and why they do it.

Reflective practice thus implies a dynamic way of being inside and outside the classroom. Teachers constantly reflect-*in*-action by pausing during their professional experiences to make sense of them and reframe them if necessary toward desired outcomes. Also, teachers constantly reflect-*on*-action by reflecting on experiences after professional events to draw insights that can help inform future practices. Teachers constantly reflect-*for*-action by becoming aware of the self within unfolding moments in their professional lives, which leads to more proactive decision-making for future teaching.

Reflective practice moves a teacher from a position of having new knowledge and awareness of espoused theories and theories-in-use to a position of using this knowledge as an informed decision maker. The final realization of this approach to reflective practice sees teachers constructing and reconstructing their own theories of practice. In this way, teachers can take full responsibility for their actions both inside and outside the classroom.

> **REFLECTIVE BREAK**
>
> - Try to answer the following questions for your reflection-for-action:
>   — What kind of teacher am I now?
>   — What kind of teacher do I want to be?
>   — Where do I see myself in five years' time? How will I get there?

References

Basturkmen, H. (2012). Review of research into the correspondence between language teachers' stated beliefs and practices. *System, 40*(2), 282–295.

Borg, S. (2003). Teacher cognition in language teaching: A review of research on what language teachers think, know, believe and do. *Language Teaching, 36*, 81–109.

Burns, A., & Richards, J. C. (Eds.). (2009). *The Cambridge guide to second language teacher education.* New York, NY: Cambridge University Press.

Dewey, J. (1933). *How we think.* Madison, WI: University of Wisconsin Press

Farrell, T. S. C. (2007). *Reflective language teaching: From research to practice.* London, England: Continuum Press.

Farrell, T. S. C. (2011). Exploring the professional role identities of experienced ESL teachers through reflective practice. *System, 66,* 1–9.

Farrell, T. S. C. (2013). *Reflective writing for language teachers.* London, England: Equinox.

Knezedivc, B. (2001). Action research. *IATEFL Teacher Development SIG Newsletter, 1,* 10–12.

Kumaravadivelu, B. (2003). *Beyond methods: Macrostrategies for language teaching.* New Haven, CT: Yale University Press.

Kumaravadivelu, B. (2012). *Language teacher education for a global society.* New York, NY: Routledge.

Oberg, A., & Blades, C. (1990). The spoken and the unspoken: The story of an educator. *Phenomonology+Pedagogy, 8,* 161–180.

Richards, J. C., & Farrell, T. S. C. (2005). *Professional development for language teachers.* New York, NY: Cambridge University Press.

Schön, D. A. (1983). *The reflective practitioner: How professionals think in action.* New York, NY: Basic Books.

Schön, D. A. (1987). *Educating the reflective practitioner: Towards a new design for teaching and learning in the profession.* San Francisco, CA: Jossey-Bass.

Stanley, C. (1998). A framework for teacher reflectivity. *TESOL Quarterly, 32,* 584–591.

Woods, D. (1996). *Teacher cognition in language teaching.* Cambridge, England: Cambridge University Press.

Zahorik, J. A. (1986). Acquiring teaching skills. *Journal of Teacher Education, 37,* 21–25.

Zeichner, K., & Liston, O. (1996). *Reflective teaching.* Hillsdale, NJ: Lawrence Erlbaum.

Also Available in the English Language Teacher Development Series

Reflective Teaching (Thomas S. C. Farrell)

Teaching Listening (Ekaterina Nemtchinova)

Teaching Pronunciation (John Murphy)

Language Classroom Assessment (Liying Cheng)

Cooperative Learning and Teaching (George Jacobs & Harumi Kimura)

Classroom Research for Language Teachers (Tim Stewart)

Teaching Digital Literacies (Joel Bloch)

Teaching Reading (Richard Day)

Teaching Grammar (William Crawford)

Teaching Vocabulary (Michael Lessard-Clouston)

Teaching Writing (Zuzana Tomas, Ilka Kostka, & Jennifer A. Mott-Smith)

English Language Teachers as Administrators (Dan Tannacito)

Content-Based Instruction (Margo Dellicarpini & Orlando Alonso)

Teaching English as an International Language
(Ali Fuad Selvi & Bedrettin Yazan)

Teaching Speaking (Tasha Bleistein, Melissa K. Smith, & Marilyn Lewis)

www.tesol.org/bookstore
tesolpubs@brightkey.net
Request a copy for review
Request a Distributor Policy